Gin & Tonic

Phoebe Stuckes

smith|doorstop

Published 2017 by
smith|doorstop books
The Poetry Business
Bank Street Arts
32-40 Bank Street
Sheffield S1 2DS

ISBN 978-1-910367-98-8
Typeset by Utter
Printed by Biddles Books

smith|doorstop books are a member of Inpress:
www.inpressbooks.co.uk. Distributed by NBN International, Airport Business
Centre, 10 Thornbury Road Plymouth PL 6 7PP

The Poetry Business gratefully acknowledges the support
of Arts Council England.

Supported by
ARTS COUNCIL
ENGLAND

Contents

To my mum

Three spells

Lost boys, go home
I like my boring life.
I'm hard as silver
and you are a fleshy blood thing.
Get out of my hands
and my inbox.

Mother deliver me from gin headaches,
I've lost enough Sunday mornings
as it is. I've written enough
thank you notes and apology letters
now is the time
for manifestos and songs.

Girl, have a peppermint tea
and sleep on it.
Keep hold of your story
like a dog on a lead.
Trust me, you'll burn through
these months like sage.

Crisis

I don't like church
as much as I enjoy incense and guilt.
I can get the same effect

from sticks of sandalwood
and reading articles online
about natural disasters

while I'm in my underwear
eating tortilla chips out of the bag.
I only like the kind of cults

where you can talk about your feelings
and grow neat rows of vegetables,
salad in allotments

while wearing soft fabrics.
My father told me all the prophets
were reluctant prophets.

They wanted to be left alone
with their homes and their families.
Then God came along

and shook up their lives
like a snowglobe,
some of them died.

I know the Church of England
Standard Worship from beginning to end,
but I could also recite Dark Side of The Moon,

if anyone cared to ask me.
I think both will be lodged in my head
forever and ever. Amen.

Ghosts

Lately I've been getting to know
the ghosts in your kitchen.
Mostly when you're answering emails
or deep in conversation with the cat.
By the counter, one strums your guitar,
one picks up your favourite books
flicks through, and drops them.
Drums her nails on the table
you re-painted yourself.
By the window, one is applying
red lip gloss to her mouth and pouting.
This one is covered in hairpin scars
and tends to keep you up past twelve
with work in the morning, with a noise
like a siren, that never quite leaves you alone.
This is where they prefer to congregate
and talk, though of course
they can walk through walls.
One plaits my hair, one says
I don't know you like they do.
Your kitchen is crowded, imagine
that many birthdays to remember,
so many phone numbers pinned
to a narrow wall.

Monologue

I'm not shivering.
Once this breeze drops, I'll be fine.
Give me two paracetamol and a week
I'll be fine. I can't face another doctor,
another cul de sac. I'm not coming back

to my parents. I can't remember
what I used to be like or what I did yesterday.
I'm sorry I kept your book for so long
I'm sorry I met you
and flirted, and never texted you back

you poor thing. Buy me another
and I'll take you home, I'll make you
believe in the sound of your voice
in the movement of your hands.
Other people's insecurities are so

romantic to me. I haven't worked on my essays
but I'm going out anyway.
This dress makes me feel
like I could be loved. I'm starving
for something. Kebab shop chips

or a gin and tonic.
I'm wilting in this heat like blossom.
I'm turning the corner
to another accident and emergency.
I could hurt myself but I probably won't.

Blues

I'm usually on my way to the library
or another hospital.

Filling in a questionnaire,
or watching the clock

for my appointment.
I've been mad for years.

I retain the ability to text
and go on the internet.

On most days I can feed myself;
stir tomatoes around a frying pan,

wind spaghetti around a fork.
Though the dishes can go untouched for weeks.

Sometimes I can even go out of the flat
and walk down the street.

It will be summer soon.
It's only a matter of time

before I fall for someone else unavailable.
My mother thinks I should come home

at the weekends.
Perhaps I should get more exercise

Perhaps I should get diagnosed.
You don't know what I've done in the small hours.

You don't know
what I've done to cope.

Home

If I'm left alone
I get swamped by the urge
to cut off my hair
or dye it an unnatural colour
one-handed, in the sink.

I want to wear black
but getting dressed feels
like being stood up.
I've a date with nothing.

I am swallowing endless photos
of exes in foreign countries
or at festivals. I suffocate my heart
in pasta and cheese sauce,
leave the dishes submerged

in rock pools of soap.
If I google how to know
if you're having a breakdown
the links are all purple.
Outside, seagulls are hooting

like ambulances.
I don't trust myself enough
to open an upstairs window
to watch them wheeling around.

Judgement

There were times I have crawled
into the space between my bed and the floor
and wouldn't come out until my heartbeat slowed
from a sprint to a pace. Remember you were lost too
but you said hey, you're the one under a bed.
Your girlfriend's underwear lined the radiators
in your flat. The night a smile tugged the corner
of your mouth like knicker elastic.
You were the only person I was not afraid
to sleep next to and it made me furious
and very frightened. I caught the scent
of your laundry powder on the street
and stayed there for minutes,
pulling you out of my heart
in handfuls, like algae from a river.
Another night you told me
to just lie there, and afterwards
that we should draw a line under it
well this is it, this is that line.

Home

I'm usually hanging around
in dressing gowns.
Buttering toast and calling a friend
to complain about poetry
or the government.

It's a rough time to be young
or to care about anything.
So I keep wandering through London
looking for something to do.

I rattle around these streets
like an urban fox.
In my second hand fur
eating junk out of polystyrene.

I don't like to follow
the thick grey artery that leads
to my flat, where I live with myself.
I tell myself that crying in cabs

could be glamorous
if I did it correctly.
I am doing my best
with bad nights and bad love.
Honey it's difficult.

Dinner

I have chewed my lip bloody
trying not to be in love with you.

I wear all the marks of the wounded,
the soft grey jumper, the ringless fingers.

I've cried about you in every major
fast food chain, and on all my bus routes

Today I realised our miseries are
incompatible. I cannot blame

how I told you I have crawled into bed
with a box of chips. Or the few

occasions you have seen me naked
for why we are not together.

How could I have known
you were expecting to chase

my sadness off? Or when you couldn't
we would stop having dinner?

That final time was enough to ruin
my favourite restaurant, which is one

of three things I cannot forgive you for.
The second is putting ketchup

on your mac and cheese, the third is burning
my house down and leaving me in it.

Look at me now

Talking about it
is like trying
to recover

a dead language.
There is nowhere
I can point to

on my body.
The clothes I wore
have been bagged up

and thrown out.
I am still married
to your likeness,

I find you
serving cookies
in Paddington Station,

ordering drinks
in New Cross Inn.
A strand of hair,

an eyelash is enough
to reduce me to panic.
I am recovered,

like a mermaid
washed up on land.
Integrated

into a standing,
talking society.
If I could, I would

draw a line as long
as four years.
Look how far

I have walked
from where you left me.
Look at me now,

sleeping with other people.
Laying down
with the enemy,

encouraging them
to touch me
in all the same ways

you did, never once
allowing them
to walk me back home.

Holding flowers in the sexual health clinic

I have done my time on blue vinyl sofas
with the stuffing falling out. I have sat
on enough wooden seats that are bolted
together, filling in forms, so that it feels
strange to be the one accompanying. Tulips
in one hand, a hand in the other. I think of
the morning I should have come here,
when instead I slept. I turned myself
to the wall, like the portrait of someone
who'd done something terrible. I was lucky,
it could have been worse. There is no
other way to consider this. When I see
those women who are huge like the Earth,
my first thought is *worse worse worse*.

Advice For Girls

Vanilla based perfumes drive men wild,
we have no evidence for this. Sudocrem
is good for spots, cuts, grazes, rashes
and sadness. Always accompany your friend
to the clinic. Boyfriends cannot be trusted
in this matter. Eyebrows are sisters not twins,
let this knowledge free you. Get a hot water bottle
for period pain, buy your own chocolate,
boyfriends cannot be trusted in this matter.
Nail varnish can be used to stop tights laddering,
if your tights ladder you cannot keep wearing them,
no it is not *Punk*. Get someone to help when dyeing
your hair, blot your lipstick. Don't borrow mascara
from women you don't trust. Text me when you get home,
keep your hand on the door in the back of the taxi.
I found his Facebook, I'm friends with his sister's
best friend's zumba instructor. Dairy makes you fat,
gluten is evil but we don't know how or why or what it is.
Beyonce, Beyonce, Beyonce.

Sugar

I have accidentally loved
several rich girls. When I found out
one was dating some boy wonder
rock star, as well as me, I considered
lifting some art from her parents'
walls and starting a better life
for myself in a new city. I could never
have a sugar daddy because I don't
look after myself. I chew at my own
fingers, and lick knives at dinner
there is an inch of brown hair
on my head that is eating
the blonde, like a snake
I am shedding my old self. I used
to say money didn't matter
now I would give anything
to be wrapped up in cash like a thick
fur coat on my naked body. If you must cry
it's better to do so in the back of a ferrari.

Imminent Catastrophe

I don't want to be someone
who believes in the stars but
when Mercury started going
backwards my mother spilt
sugar all over the kitchen floor
and when I spoke to a girlfriend
on Skype she froze, her face a ghost-orb
while I cried out hello hello and she
could hear me but I couldn't hear her.
My birthday is between the lion
and the virgin which explains
why I am constantly running between
draining other people's blood and
shedding my own. I don't want
to believe it but sometimes the moon
comes down from her mezzanine and she
predicts imminent catastrophe and that
I should steer clear of redhead girls.

Flotsam

I lost a skateboard in a break up,
I was young.

Some people hoard
what they think you've abandoned.

In this way I've lost
a skull print t-shirt,

a scallop shell
on a silver chain.

They sometimes
leave flotsam behind.

I threw out a bra
that hung like bunting

from the edge of the dustbin
for a week,

a pair of pants
I should have burned

like the flag of a fallen regime.
Does everyone go home

missing something?
I myself have stolen

some wool-rich, Marks and Spencers
socks, the morning after Valentines

when my shoes made me bleed.
I kept an earring

that sometimes spikes me
from the bottom of my purse,

and headphones I was given
already broken. They crackle and whine

like a person with a feeling
they are struggling to express.

Little Song

I think of tattoos like love or childbirth:
if it were that painful, everyone would stop.
We could get by on goldfish and biros,
squares of wax paper that sponge on a mark.
I don't believe that everything worthwhile
takes commitment. Takes waiting rooms
and what must be foolishness. Take this girl,
first doodled by Picasso on a napkin
maybe, then drawn into my arm with needles
one bent-up Wednesday. She reminds me of you,
how you clutched my hand in the clinic, your nails
digging into my palms, before the nurse came
to take you away. How we both say that it hurt
and anyone who says otherwise is lying.

Feathers

Remember me or don't.
I have told the whole town about you.
They are lining up to feather me
for what you did, but I'm dancing circles
around them. You cannot touch me.
You call but the noise
at the other end is your own
cry for help. The trick came off.
The assistant was the magician
all along, now she's a dove,
flitting off into the sunset.
I left that girl
curled up in one half
of the box you sawed apart.
I am altered, if you saw me
on the street I couldn't
be recognised. My body is Picasso's
Guernica. My eyes are the cold
centre of a flame.
Look on your works
and worry about it.

Mad Chicks Cool

A mad chick is a bloodstain on a white skirt.
She has no mother of her own but gave birth
to herself in a shell or a dustbin. Every time
you cut off the head of a mad chick, two more
sprout in her place. Men want to fuck us
but wouldn't spit on a mad chick if she
was on fire. Right now, a mad chick
is cosying up to your girlfriend on a velvet
chaise longue. Your new boss is a mad chick,
perhaps your mother was a mad chick
which is why you hate them now. Watch out,
the mad chicks are in the street outside,
ripping up the pavement with their tombstone
teeth, smashing shop fronts with their wings,
now there is nothing in this world that can stop them.

Acknowledgements

I would like to thank the editors at the following publications for including my work: 'Three Spells' in *Ambit 223*, 'Crisis' in *Rising 65*, 'Ghosts' in the *Wenlock Poetry Festival Anthology 2016*, 'Advice for Girls' online as a commended winner of the Troubadour Prize, 'Imminent Catastrophe' in *An Orchestra of Feathers and Bone* the Barbican Young Poets Anthology 2017, 'Little Song' in *HWAET! 20 Years of Ledbury Poetry Festival*.

Endless thanks is due to the Foyle Young Poets Award and The Poetry Society for their support of my work from a young age, in particular to Lucy Wood for always supporting my poetry and my outfits.

To Jacob Sam-La Rose, R.A Villanueva and all the Barbican Young Poets for constantly renewing my enjoyment of poetry.

To Jack Underwood and Eva Salzman for their invaluable workshops and editorial help at Goldsmiths. And of course to everyone at The Poetry Business for their tremendous work and love in putting this together.

Phoebe Stuckes was a winner of the 2015/16 New Poets Prize

The New Poets Prize is a pamphlet competition for writers between the ages of 16 and 22 (inclusive). The prize runs alongside the renowned International Book & Pamphlet Competition organised by The Poetry Business, which has been a staple of the literary calendar since 1986.

Entrants are invited to submit short collections of twelve pages of poems. Four outstanding poets will be selected to receive a year of support and mentoring alongside other prizes, including a place on an Arvon residential course and publication in *The North* magazine.

The winning collections will appear as part of The New Poets List, an imprint of The Poetry Business.

Judging the New Poets Prize in 2015/16, Helen Mort said:

"When I encounter new voices so exhilarating and exact they require me to listen differently, to attend properly, it's a rare thrill. Judging the New Poets Prize yielded many such moments of surprise and delight."

In association with Arvon. Supported by Arts Council England

Also published by smith|doorstop in the
New Poets List:

JENNY DANES, GAPS

*Gaps' is full of anthropological, elegantly-crafted poems that stand
back and take a good, hard look around the room, finding a fresh
language for what they see: 'darkness comes and holds me like a glove,
/ which, by next morning, is a fist'. Poems about moving countries,
poems about love, poems about the gaps in language...every subject is
treated with clear-sighted confidence.*

– Helen Mort

Gaps speaks about the gaps between two different languages and
cultures, and questions how successfully love can bridge these. It's
also about uncomfortable spaces: the distance between your desired
self and your true self, between anxiety and reality, between your
body and another person's body.

Jenny Danes was born in Chelmsford in 1995 and studies English
Literature and German at Newcastle University. In 2013 and 2016
she was highly commended in the Bridport Prize for poetry and
in 2016 she won The Poetry Business New Poets Prize. Her work
has appeared in various magazines including *The Rialto, Magma,
The North, Brittle Star, The Missing Slate* and *The Cadaverine*.

Gaps is published by smith|doorstop
Order it now from the shop at http://www.poetrybusiness.co.uk

THEOPHILUS KWEK, THE FIRST FIVE STORMS

The First Five Storms' has remarkable range and imaginative depth, from Fibonacci to Loch na Fuaiche, from the small detail of 'thawed streams like cracks in the bone' to a panorama of the whole 'lifting land'. These are poems that excavate, honour and renew.

– Helen Mort

Theophilus Kwek is 22 and studying for a MSc in Refugee and Forced Migration Studies in Oxford. He has published three collections of poetry, most recently Giving Ground (2016). He won the Martin Starkie Prize in 2014, the Jane Martin Prize in 2015, and the New Poets' Prize in 2016, and was recently placed Second in the Stephen Spender Prize for Poetry in Translation, 2016. Having served as President of the Oxford University Poetry Society, he is the Co-Founder of The Kindling and a Co-Editor of Oxford Poetry. Having recently arrived in a country best-known for its weather, he charts the storms of history, language, place, and tradition in *The First Five Storms*.

The First Five Storms is published by smith|doorstop
Order it now from the shop at http://www.poetrybusiness.
co.uk

IMOGEN CASSELS, THE FIRE MANIFESTO

The Fire Manifesto is full of praise-poems, poems that celebrate the detail of 'the moon reflecting on the sea', the ritual of making bread, the 'scalloped edge' of land. But the praising is never naïve – many of these poems have a haunted, haunting quality too. Knowing and sorrowful, the writing is subtle, always attentive to the music of names.

– Helen Mort

Imogen Cassels is from Sheffield, and is in her second year studying English at Cambridge. In 2015 she was selected as a Young Poet on the Underground. Her poetry is published or forthcoming in *Blackbox Manifold*, *Waymaking*, *Ambit*, *The Interpreter's House*, and *Antiphon*.

Imogen Cassels' pamphlet is forthcoming from smith|doorstop. Keep a look out for it at http://www.poetrybusiness.co.uk